Introduction to the world of influencer and content creater marketing

Influencer marketing is a form of online marketing in which companies work with so-called influencers to promote their products or services. An influencer is a person who has a large number of followers on social media platforms such as Instagram, TikTok, YouTube or others and is therefore able to spread their opinions and recommendations. Influencer marketing can be very effective for businesses because influencers often have a loyal and engaged fan base that trusts them and listens to their recommendations. By collaborating with influencers, companies can showcase their products or services to a wide audience while building a personal connection with their potential customers. There are different types of influencer marketing campaigns, from sponsored posts and product reviews to collaborations and long-term partnerships. The type of campaign depends on the company's goals and the type of product or service. However, it is important to note that influencer marketing also presents some challenges. One of them is the credibility of the influencers, as there have been some cases of fake recommendations and paid reviews in the past. Therefore, it is important for companies to carefully consider which influencers they work with and ensure that the campaign is transparent and authentic. Overall, influencer marketing can be an effective strategy for creating awareness for a brand and reaching potential customers. However, it requires thorough planning and implementation to ensure the campaign is successful and expectations are met.

History of influencer marketing

Influencer marketing is a relatively new concept, originating in the early days of the social media age. It started in the late 2000s when more and more people logged onto social networks like Facebook and Twitter and started sharing their opinions and experiences with others. In 2010, Instagram was launched, a platform focused on visual content such as photos and videos.

Instagram quickly became a success and became the preferred place for users to share their personal photos. Over time, it also became a place for celebrities and other influential figures to build their own brand. It didn't take long for companies to become aware of the potential of influencers and start using them for marketing purposes. The first known case of influencer marketing dates back to 2006, when the company PayPerPost was launched. This company offered bloggers money to write about and link to their products. However, there was no expression for this type of marketing at the time. The term "influencer marketing" first emerged in the early 2010s to describe the practice of using social media personalities to promote products or services. In the early years of influencer marketing, it was primarily celebrities who were used as influencers. However, that quickly changed as more and more "normal" people built up large followings and became influencers. Today, influencer marketing is an important part of many companies' marketing strategy. Companies work with influencers to promote their product or service and increase their reach. Influencers often receive money or free product in return. The story of influencer marketing is far from over as the social media landscape is constantly changing and evolving. The future of influencer marketing will likely be influenced by new platforms, technologies and trends.

Different species and niches

Influencers are people who have built a following through their presence on social media and other digital channels and can influence those followers. There are many different types of influencers operating in different niches. Here are some examples: Beauty influencers: These influencers are known for their beauty and skin care tips. They showcase products such as makeup, skin care products, hair products and perfumes. Fitness Influencers: These influencers specialize in fitness and health and provide advice on workouts, nutrition, and lifestyle. You can also promote products like fitness equipment, nutritional supplements, and fitness apparel. Fashion Influencers: These influencers are experts in fashion and styling and present the latest trends and styles. You can promote products like clothing, shoes, accessories, and jewelry. Travel Influencers: These influencers share their travels and adventures and provide tips and recommendations on travel destinations, accommodations and activities. You can also promote products like travel equipment, hotels, and airlines. Lifestyle influencers: These influencers showcase their lives and interests and can promote a wider range of products, including technology, kitchen accessories, books and music. Gaming Influencers: These influencers specialize in video games and show gameplay, give advice on gaming hardware and software, and promote products like gaming accessories and clothing. Parenting influencers: These influencers share their experiences and advice as parents and promote products such as children's clothing, toys and baby gear. Food Influencers: These influencers are food experts and provide advice on recipes, restaurants, and nutrition. You can also promote products like kitchen appliances and groceries. Business Influencers: These influencers specialize in business and careers and provide advice on leadership, entrepreneurship, and human resources. You can also promote products like office supplies and business software. These are just a few examples of the many types of influencers and their niches. However, there are many other categories of influencers, such as music influencers, art influencers and political influencers.

How to plan a successful campaign

Planning a successful influencer campaign requires a few steps and strategies. Here are some steps you can follow: Identify Audience: Identify your audience and who you want to reach. Determine the age, interests and demographics of your target audience. Set Budget: Determine your budget and how much you want to spend on your campaign. Select influencers: Identify the appropriate influencers for your campaign. Make sure the influencers fit your product or brand and that their target audience is also your target audience. Plan content: Develop a strategy for the content you want to create. Provide guidance to influencers so they know exactly what type of content you need. Create a schedule: Set a schedule for your campaign, including when the content will be published and when the campaign will run. Measuring results: Set KPIs (Key Performance Indicators) to measure the success of your campaign. This can include the number of views, comments, shares and sales. Negotiate Contracts: Create a written agreement that sets out the expectations and responsibilities of both parties. Follower engagement: Create incentives for followers to actively participate in the campaign, for example by using hashtags or entering a contest. Follow-up: Track the progress of your campaign and adjust your strategy if necessary. By following these steps, you can plan and execute a successful influencer campaign that appeals to your target audience and promotes your brand.

How to choose the right influencer

Influencer marketing is a popular marketing strategy that allows companies to promote their products or services by collaborating with influencers who have a large following on social media. Choosing the right influencer can help your business achieve greater reach and engagement. Here are some tips to choose the right influencer: Target audience: Make sure the influencer has a similar audience to your company. You want to make sure your message gets to the right people. Relevance: Check whether the influencer is relevant in your field and has the necessary expertise to effectively promote your brand. Authenticity: Look for an influencer who is authentic and communicates with their following in an honest and credible way. Engagement: Check the influencer's engagement rate to ensure they have an active and engaged following. Quality: Make sure the influencer produces high-quality content that fits your business. Budget: Consider your budget when choosing an influencer. Some influencers charge higher fees than others. Check Reputation: Check the influencer's reputation to make sure he or she doesn't have any controversies or scandals that could negatively impact your brand. By considering these factors, you can choose the right influencer who can help your business achieve its goals.

How to successfully build a relationship with influencers

Building a successful relationship with influencers can be very important for brands and companies to expand their reach and promote their products or services. Here are some tips that can help you build a successful relationship with influencers: Identify the right influencer: Choose an influencer who fits your brand or product and whose audience overlaps with your potential customers. You can search social media platforms like Instagram, YouTube, or TikTok to find influencers who are active in your niche. Get in touch: Once you've identified an influencer you want to reach out to, you can send a personal message or email the influencer. It's important to be polite and respectful and to clearly communicate your goals and expectations. Offer a clear collaboration: Make the influencer an offer that is mutually beneficial. It could be a paid collaboration where the influencer promotes your products or services, or a partnership where you provide free products or services to the influencer. Establish trust: A successful relationship with an influencer requires trust. You can earn the influencer's trust by being authentic, transparent, and sticking to your promises. Set clear goals: Set clear goals that you want to achieve through the collaboration. This could include increasing your reach, improving your brand image or increasing sales. Communicate regularly: It is important to stay in regular contact with the influencer to ensure the collaboration goes smoothly. Make sure you set clear expectations and deadlines for collaboration and keep the influencer updated. Promote the influencer: If you have had a successful collaboration with an influencer, you can help him or her expand his or her own reach by sharing his or her work and recommending him or her to other brands or companies.

How to develop a successful marketing strategy

Influencer marketing can be an extremely effective strategy for spreading the word about your brand or products and attracting customers. Here are some steps you can follow to develop a successful influencer marketing strategy: Define Audience: Determine who your target audience is and which influencers influence them. Consider demographics, interests, behaviors and locations. Also identify the type of content your target audience prefers. Set Goals: Set clear and measurable goals you want to achieve with your influencer marketing campaign. Examples of goals can include: increasing brand awareness, increasing sales, or increasing social media followers. Set a budget: Set a realistic budget for your campaign based on the cost of engaging with influencers and creating content. Find influencers: Identify influencers who appeal to your target audience and align with your brand. Consider the size of their follower base, engagement rate and the quality of their content. Use tools like Social Blade to verify the authenticity of influencers. Agree on collaboration: Agree on collaboration with the influencers and define clear expectations and contractual terms. Make sure influencers fully understand what is expected of them and what benefits and considerations are provided. Create content: Develop a content strategy for your campaign and create engaging and relevant content that appeals to your target audience. Make sure the content reflects your brand's tone and style guidelines and is high quality. Run Campaign: Implement your influencer marketing campaign and promote it on various social media platforms. Monitor your campaign's performance and adjust if necessary. Measure and optimize: Use tools like Google Analytics to measure and track the success of your campaign. Optimize your campaign based on the insights gained and continually improve your influencer marketing strategy. By following these steps, you can develop a successful influencer marketing strategy that will help promote your brand and reach your target audience.

How to measure the success of a campaign

Measuring the success of an influencer campaign can be done in a variety of ways, depending on the campaign's goals and available resources. Here are some key metrics and tools that can be used to measure the success of an influencer campaign: Engagement Rate: Engagement rate measures how actively viewers respond to the influencer's content, including likes, comments, and shares. A higher engagement rate means the influencer's content is better received and potentially has a greater impact. Impressions and Reach: Impressions measure how many times the influencer's content has been viewed, while reach is the number of people who have seen that content. A higher reach means that the campaign has reached a larger target group. Conversions: A conversion is an action that a viewer takes as a result of the campaign, such as a purchase, registration or login. Measuring conversions can be an indication of whether the campaign is actually having an impact on the behavior of the target group. Brand awareness: Brand awareness measures how many people knew the brand before they heard about the campaign compared to those who knew the brand after. This metric can be used to determine whether the campaign helped increase brand awareness. Social Listening Tools: Social listening tools can be used to measure audience sentiment and determine whether the campaign had a positive or negative impact on the brand image. It is important to set clear goals and metrics before starting the campaign to measure the success of the campaign. By tracking the metrics above, you can determine how effective the campaign was and what changes should be made to improve future campaigns.

The importance of content quality in influencer marketing

Content quality plays a very important role in influencer marketing. As influencers, people or groups of people (such as bloggers, YouTubers, Instagrammers) present content to reach and influence their followers. The quality of the content is crucial to whether the target group is reached and positively influenced. An important aspect of content quality in influencer marketing is authenticity. Followers expect influencers to be honest and transparent, and to only promote products or services that they use or believe in. If the content is not authentic, this will be recognized by followers and can lead to a loss of trust. Another important aspect is the relevance of the content for the target group. The content must be tailored to the interests and needs of the target audience in order to capture their attention and influence them. If the content is not relevant, the target audience is likely to ignore it. The quality of the visual and textual representation also plays a role. The content must be aesthetically pleasing and well-written to grab the audience's attention and leave a positive impression. Overall, content quality in influencer marketing is a crucial factor for the success of an influencer campaign. If the content is authentic, relevant and aesthetically pleasing, it can reach and influence the target audience, resulting in a positive perception of the advertised products or services.

How to Use Influencer Marketing on Social Media

Influencer marketing is a strategy in which companies work with influencers (people with a large following on social media) to promote their products or services. Here are some steps that companies should consider if they want to use influencer marketing on social media: Identify suitable influencers: Think about who your target audience is and which influencers might influence them. Look for influencers who are already talking about your company or industry or who share similar interests and values. Setting Goals and KPIs: Determine what you want to achieve with the influencer marketing campaign, such as increasing awareness or increasing sales. Also determine the KPIs (Key Performance Indicators) that you will use to measure the success of the campaign. Develop a campaign strategy: Think about what type of content and actions influencers will share in your campaigns to achieve your goals. This can also include competitions or exclusive offers. Arrange a collaboration: Contact the influencer and talk about collaboration. Determine the details such as compensation, collaboration timeframe, and type of content the influencer will create. Monitor and measure success: Track campaign performance against your KPIs and monitor how the influencer promotes your brand or product. Adjust your strategy if necessary. Cultivate long-term relationships: Think about how you can build long-term relationships with the influencers. Long-term collaboration can help continually showcase your brand on social media and reach your target audience. Overall, influencer marketing on social media can be an effective strategy to introduce your brand or product to a wider audience and gain the trust of your target audience. However, it requires careful planning and implementation to be successful.

How to Run a Successful Influencer Marketing Campaign on Instagram

A successful influencer marketing campaign on Instagram consists of several steps. Here are some steps you can follow: Define your audience: Before you start the campaign, you should define your audience and set your goals. Who are your potential customers? What do you want to achieve? What should your campaign look like? What type of influencer do you want to use? Select influencers: Look for influencers who fit your company and your target group. Check their followers and engagement rates and make sure they have an authentic and engaged community. You can also filter influencers based on specific criteria such as interests, location, and demographics. Develop a campaign idea: Think of a creative idea for your campaign that suits both the influencer and your company. It can be a challenge, a giveaway or a collaboration with other brands. Sign a contract: Make sure you sign a contract with the influencer that specifies all the details of the collaboration, including how the collaboration will work, the period and compensation. Approve content: Review the content the influencer creates to ensure it meets your brand guidelines. Publish campaign: Once the content is approved, the campaign can be started. The influencer shares the content on their profile and you can also share it on your own profile. Measure results: Measure the success of your campaign against the set goals. Check engagement rates, follower counts, sales, and other metrics relevant to your campaign. Follow-up with influencer: After the campaign is over, make sure to thank the influencer for their cooperation and provide feedback if necessary. By following these steps, you can run a successful influencer marketing campaign on Instagram. However, it is important to build a creative, authentic and long-term relationship with influencers to achieve long-term success.

How to Run a Successful Influencer Marketing Campaign on YouTube

A successful influencer marketing campaign on YouTube requires careful planning and execution. Here are some steps to follow: Select Audience and Influencers: Select an audience you want to reach and find influencers who have a high number of followers in that audience. Also check whether the influencers' values and interests align with your brand. Set campaign type and budget: Decide what type of campaign you want to run and how much you want to spend on it. Some options include product reviews, sponsored posts or integrations, contests and giveaways. Start communication with the influencer: Connect with the influencer and discuss the campaign details. Discuss what type of content they will create, how long the campaign will last, and what compensation will be offered. Create Content: The influencer creates content that relates to and highlights your brand. Make sure the content is authentic and engaging to capture the interest of the target audience. Promote the content: After the content is created, you should ensure that it is seen by the target audience. Promote them on your own social media channels and also promote them on the influencer's YouTube page. Measure campaign success: Track campaign performance and monitor key metrics such as reach, engagement and sales. Use these insights to improve your future influencer marketing campaigns. In summary, it is important to have a clear strategy, create authentic content and work closely with the influencer to run a successful influencer marketing campaign on YouTube.

How to Run a Successful Influencer Marketing Campaign on TikTok

TikTok is a social media platform where many people spend time creating and sharing content. For businesses, using influencer marketing on TikTok can be a great way to reach their target audience. Here are some steps that businesses should follow to run a successful influencer marketing campaign on TikTok: Define Audience: Before launching a campaign, businesses need to know their target audience. This allows the selection of the influencer who will run the campaign to be better tailored to the target group. Select an influencer: Companies should choose an influencer who has a large and engaged following on TikTok. The influencer should also be able to communicate the company's desired message in an authentic and engaging way. Set campaign goal: Companies should set clear and specific goals for the campaign. These goals may include increasing brand awareness, promoting a product, or increasing sales of products. Create content: Together with the influencer, the company should develop a concept for the content of the campaign. The content should be targeted to the target group and the campaign goal. Run campaign: Once the content has been created, the campaign can be started. The influencer should upload the content to their TikTok page and share it on other social media platforms if necessary. Measure campaign performance: Companies should monitor campaign performance to see if it achieved its goals. This can be done by monitoring metrics such as number of views, likes and comments. Reward influencers: Companies should reward influencers for their work. This can be in the form of financial compensation or free products. It's important to note that a successful influencer marketing campaign on TikTok takes time and effort. Companies should ensure that they are working with an experienced influencer and are willing to invest in the campaign to achieve the desired results.

How to Run a Successful Influencer Marketing Campaign on LinkedIn

LinkedIn is a great platform for influencer marketing campaigns because it focuses on professional connections and business prospecting. Here are some steps you can follow to run a successful influencer marketing campaign on LinkedIn: Audience analysis: Identify your target audience and the type of content that interests them. Think about who might influence your business and what type of influencer would best fit your brand. Influencer research: Search for influencers on LinkedIn who appeal to your target audience. Check what posts and interactions they already have on the platform. You should also check their reach, engagement and credibility. Contact: Once you have found an influencer you would like to work with, you should make an initial contact. Make sure you communicate your intentions and expectations clearly. Work out collaboration: Once you have reached an agreement with the influencer, you should work together to develop a campaign that meets your goals and target group. Make sure you agree on the content and format the influencer will create. Measuring results: During the campaign, you should track and analyze your results. Check whether your goals were achieved and whether the collaboration with the influencer was successful. Follow-up: After the campaign, you should thank your influencer for their collaboration. You can also collect feedback to improve future campaigns. Overall, it's important to ensure your influencer campaign is authentic and targeted to your target audience. By following these steps, you can run a successful influencer marketing campaign on LinkedIn.

How to Run a Successful Influencer Marketing Campaign on Twitter

A successful influencer marketing campaign on Twitter involves careful planning, execution, and analysis. Here are some steps you can follow to run a successful campaign: Define your goals and audience: Before you begin, you need to define your goals and audience. Do you want to increase your awareness, drive more traffic to your website or increase your sales? Who is your target group and what are their interests? Identify relevant influencers: Find influencers who have a high number of followers and are active in your field. Look for influencers who appeal to your target audience and have a high engagement rate. Create a plan: Create a plan for your campaign, including the content you want to create with the influencer, the duration of the campaign, and the budget. Collaborate with the influencer: Work with the influencer to create the content and ensure it appropriately represents your brand. Use relevant hashtags to spread your campaign content. Track your results: Track your results and analyze them regularly. Measure your performance using metrics such as number of impressions, clicks, retweets, likes and conversions. Optimize your campaign:

Based on your results, optimize and adjust your campaign. Make changes that help improve performance and achieve your goals. In summary, it is important to plan your campaign carefully, identify relevant influencers, create a clear plan, work closely with the influencer, track your results and optimize your campaign. By following these steps, you can run a successful influencer marketing campaign on Twitter.

How to Run a Successful Influencer Marketing Campaign on Pinterest

Pinterest is an excellent platform for influencer marketing campaigns as it allows businesses to share visual content and connect with an active community. Here are some steps you can follow to run a successful influencer marketing campaign on Pinterest: Define your target audience: Identify your target audience to ensure you work with the right influencers and tailor your campaign on Pinterest to their needs and interests align. Select influencers: Select the influencers who best fit your product or brand and have an engaged following on Pinterest. Make sure you look closely at the influencer's work to make sure it's a suitable collaboration. Create a campaign hashtag: Create a unique hashtag for your campaign that you can use with any Pins created as part of the campaign. This will help promote your campaign and measure success. Create campaign content: Create visually appealing content that targets your audience and conveys your brand's message. Share this content with influencers and ask them to pin it to their boards. Collaborate with influencers: Make sure the influencers you work with have enough freedom to create authentic content tailored to their followers. Also give them instructions on how to incorporate the hashtag and your brand into their Pins. Monitor and Measure: Monitor campaign progress and measure success using engagement rates, click-through rates, and other key metrics. Use this information to improve your future campaigns. By following these steps, you can run a successful influencer marketing campaign on Pinterest and showcase your brand to a wide audience.

How to Run a Successful Influencer Marketing Campaign on Snapchat

Running a successful influencer marketing campaign on Snapchat requires careful planning and execution. Here are some steps to consider: Audience Identification: Identify the audience you want to target. Research what type of content is popular on Snapchat and who the audience is that consumes that content. Influencer Selection: Choose an influencer who has a strong presence on Snapchat and whose audience matches your target audience. You can find an influencer through influencer marketing platforms like CreatorIQ or Influencer.co. Make agreements: Create an agreement with the influencer that specifies the scope of cooperation, payment and other important details. Create campaign concept: Develop a creative concept for the campaign that highlights the brand and product. Make sure it works well on Snapchat, for example by using face filters, lenses or stickers. Implement the campaign: The influencer then creates Snapchat content according to the concept to promote the campaign and shares it with their followers. You can also run sponsored content to increase campaign visibility. Review results: Track the results of the campaign and analyze how successful it was. Use data like reach, engagement, and conversion rate to optimize future campaigns. Through careful planning and execution, you can run a successful influencer marketing campaign on Snapchat that captures the attention of your target audience and strengthens your brand.

How to Use Influencer Marketing for B2B Businesses

Influencer marketing is a marketing strategy in which a brand partners with a person or group of people who has a large following on social media or other online platforms. These people, called "influencers," can help increase a brand's visibility and credibility by getting their products or services in front of their following. Although influencer marketing is often associated with B2C companies, it can also be beneficial for B2B companies. Here are some tips on how B2B companies can use influencer marketing: Identify the right influencers: Identify people or groups who are active in your industry or niche and have a large following. Consider not only the number of followers, but also their influence and credibility. Develop a strategy: Develop a strategy for your collaboration with influencers. Think about what type of content best suits your business and goals, and how you can best reach the influencer's following. Provide valuable content: Provide the influencer with valuable content that he or she can share with their following. This could be, for example, exclusive insights into your products or services, white papers or studies. Use different platforms: Influencers are active on different platforms. Consider which platforms your target audience is most likely to be active on and develop your content accordingly. Measure success: Measure the success of your influencer marketing campaign using metrics like engagement rate, reach, and conversions. Use these insights to optimize your future campaigns. Overall, influencer marketing can be an effective marketing strategy for B2B companies to increase their visibility and credibility and attract new customers.

How to Use Influencer Marketing for Nonprofit Organizations

Influencer marketing can be an effective way for non-profit organizations to spread their messages and raise funds. Here are some steps you can follow to use influencer marketing for your nonprofit organization: Identify suitable influencers: Look for influencers who fit the topic of your organization and who have a high reach in your target group. Offer Incentives: Influencers are often paid for their work or receive other incentives, such as products or services. If you are a nonprofit organization, you can offer these incentives in the form of donation receipts, thank you letters, or other forms of recognition. Develop a partnership: Develop a long-term partnership with influencers to ensure they identify with and are engaged with your organization. Create engaging content: Work with influencers to create engaging content that effectively conveys your messages and engages your audience. Distribute your content: Make sure your content is published on the influencer's and your organization's social media channels. Also use paid advertising to get your content in front of a larger audience. Measure success: Track your campaign performance and measure success using metrics such as reach, engagement, donations and other relevant metrics. By taking these steps, non-profit organizations can successfully use influencer marketing to spread their messages and achieve their goals.

How to Use Influencer Marketing for Retail

Influencer marketing is a strategy in which companies work with influencers to promote their products or services and reach their target audience. In retail, influencer marketing can be very effective in attracting the attention of potential customers and increasing sales. Here are some steps retail businesses can take to leverage influencer marketing: Identify relevant influencers: Find out which influencers are in your industry and have a strong following that may be interested in your products. Examine their profiles and see what type of content they create and how engaged their followers are. Decide to Collaborate: Identify the influencers you want to work with and decide what type of campaign best suits your business. Possible options include paid posts, affiliate programs, product reviews or giveaways. Develop a campaign: Create a strategy that targets your campaign's goals, such as increasing brand awareness, increasing sales, or introducing new products. Plan the content and timeframe for collaborating with the influencer. Track campaign success: Measure the success of your influencer campaign to see if it achieved your goals. Use analytics and reports to track and understand campaign results. Use the results for future campaigns: Use the insights from your campaign to improve and optimize future influencer campaigns. Learn what worked and what didn't and adjust your strategy accordingly. Overall, influencer marketing can be a very effective way for retail companies to reach their target audience and promote their products. By identifying relevant influencers, developing a strategy, and measuring campaign success, you can ensure that your influencer campaign is successful.

Influencer marketing for the travel industry

Influencer marketing is a powerful way for companies in the travel industry to promote their products and services. Here are some tips on how to use influencer marketing for the travel industry: Identify relevant influencers: Find influencers who are relevant to the travel industry's target audience, such as travel bloggers, food bloggers, adventurers or travel photographers. It's important to choose influencers who appeal to an audience interested in travel and tourism. Create a campaign: Create a campaign with clear goals that target the travel industry audience. A campaign may involve the influencer booking a trip, visiting and reporting on a specific destination, or the influencer testing and posting about a specific product or service. Make sure the influencer has an authentic voice: An influencer should be able to speak authentically and honestly about the experience he or she had with the product or service. Audiences will be skeptical if the influencer appears to be selling on sponsored content. Emphasize the benefits: When an influencer talks about a product or service, the benefits to the consumer should be emphasized. For example, emphasize the amenities of a hotel or the savings that can be achieved by booking a specific travel package. Track the results: It is important to track the results of the influencer campaign to understand whether it is successful. Track the engagement rates on the influencer's social media platforms and the number of clicks on the links the influencer shared in their posts. Based on these results, future campaigns can be optimized and adjusted. Pay attention to FTC compliance: In the US, influencers must mark their sponsored content with FTC guidelines. It is important to ensure that all sponsored content is labeled accordingly to avoid a penalty. Overall, influencer marketing for the travel industry can be a powerful way to engage audiences and increase awareness of products and services. However, it is important to create a clear campaign with a relevant influencer and ensure the influencer has an authentic voice and FTC compliance is taken into account.

Influencer marketing for the fashion industry

Influencer marketing has become an important part of the marketing mix for many companies, including the fashion industry. Here are some steps you can take to leverage influencer marketing for the fashion industry: Identify your target audience: Before you start influencer marketing, you need to define your target audience. Who are the people who want to buy your brand? What are their ages, genders, interests and locations? A clear idea of your target group will help you find the right influencers. Find the right influencers: Once you have identified your target audience, you can start searching for the right influencers. Look for influencers who have a similar audience to your brand and whose content and style align with your brand. You can find influencers through social media, influencer marketing platforms, or through personal recommendations. Plan your campaign: Before you start working with influencers, you need to plan your campaign. Determine the goal of your campaign, what type of content you want, what platforms you want to use, and what budget you have available. A clear plan will help you make your campaign more effective. Collaborate with influencers: Once you have found influencers you want to collaborate with, you need to contact them and arrange a collaboration. Set the terms and expectations of your collaboration and make sure you have a clear agreement. Influencers can help you promote your brand on their social media channels by sharing photos and videos of themselves wearing or using your products in their posts. Measure success: After your influencer campaign is complete, you should measure success to determine how effective it was. Monitor the performance of influencers' posts on their channels, how many followers they reached, how many sales they generated, how much traffic was generated on your website, and what impact it had on brand awareness. You can use this data to optimize your future campaigns. Overall, influencer marketing can be an effective tool for the fashion industry to promote their products and reach their target audience. However, it requires careful planning and collaboration to create a successful campaign.

Influencer marketing for the beauty industry

Influencer marketing is one of the most effective strategies for gaining consumer attention and interest in the beauty industry. Here are some steps businesses can take to successfully leverage influencer marketing: Identify your target audience: Before reaching out to influencers, you should know who your target audience is. Who are your customers? What are their interests and needs? Which social media platforms do they use most often? Find the right influencers: Once you know your target audience, you can look for influencers who appeal to that audience. Make sure their values and personality fit your brand and that they have a dedicated fan base. Create a clear campaign strategy: determine what goals you want to achieve with the campaign and how you will achieve them. Consider what type of content influencers should create, which hashtags they should use, and how long the campaign should run. Make sure the content is authentic: The content should not seem like an advertisement but should be authentic and relevant to the target group. Give influencers freedom to create content, but make sure they represent your brand and products properly. Measure campaign success: Monitor reach, engagement and sales to measure campaign success. Use analytics and statistics to see what content performed best and what areas can be improved. Overall, influencer marketing can be a powerful strategy to increase engagement and sales in the beauty industry. However, it is important that the campaign is carefully planned and implemented to ensure that it is authentic and relevant to the target group.

Influencer marketing for the technology industry

Influencer marketing is an effective strategy for the technology industry as it allows you to reach potential customers in an authentic way and increase awareness of your products or services. Here are some tips on how to leverage influencer marketing for the tech industry: Identify relevant influencers: Look for influencers in the tech industry who have a strong social media presence and have built an engaged community. Make sure the influencers have an audience that is relevant to your brand. Involve the influencers in your campaign: Make sure you have a clear idea of how you want to involve the influencers in your campaign. For example, you could provide them with products to try and promote on their social media. You could also ask to write guest posts for your blog or website. Rely on long-term partnerships: Long-term collaborations with influencers can help increase awareness of your brand in the long term. Consider turning influencers into brand ambassadors who regularly promote you and recommend your products or services. Measure success: Track the performance of your influencer marketing campaign. Use metrics like engagement rate, reach, and conversions to measure and optimize the success of your campaign. Be transparent: Make sure your influencers are transparent about their relationship with your brand and use tagged posts to show their followers that they are promoting your brand. Overall, influencer marketing can be an effective strategy for the technology industry to reach potential customers and increase awareness of their products or services. It's important to have a clear idea of how you want to involve influencers in your campaign, build long-term partnerships and measure success to optimize the effectiveness of your campaign.

Influencer marketing for the financial industry

Influencer marketing has become an important strategy for companies in various industries, including the financial industry. Here are some steps to successfully use influencer marketing in the financial industry: Identify relevant influencers: Identify people with a strong social media presence, who have a large number of followers and are able to make a positive impact Reach your target audience. Choose people who have a connection to the financial industry, such as financial experts, investors, entrepreneurs or people who talk about finance, economics and money. Develop a strategy: Develop a strategy aimed at engaging the target audience and gaining their trust. Consider the needs and interests of the target group and how you can address them through collaboration with the influencer. Create relevant content: Create content that targets your audience's interests and needs. For example, you can create informative blog posts, informative infographics, or entertainment videos related to the financial industry. The influencer can then share this content on their social media. Make sure you label the influencer according to applicable rules: If you work with an influencer to promote your brand or promote your products and services, it is important that you label this clearly and transparently. Many countries have specific rules for influencer marketing that you must follow. Measure your results: Measure the results of your influencer campaign to see how well it worked. For example, track the number of clicks on your content, the number of likes, comments and shares, and the number of sales directly attributable to the campaign. Overall, influencer marketing can be an effective way to gain the interest and trust of the target audience in the financial industry. By collaborating with an influencer, you can increase your reach and increase your brand awareness.

Influencer marketing for the automotive industry

Influencer marketing is an effective way for automotive companies to promote their products and services and reach their target audience. Here are some steps that can be helpful in implementing influencer marketing for the automotive industry: Identify suitable influencers: Find influencers who work in the automotive industry and have a large following. Choosing influencers that appeal to your target audience is crucial. There are specialized platforms like Hypr or Influencer.co that can help with this. Create an authentic brand experience: Give influencers enough creative freedom to present your products and services in an authentic way. The idea is to create an experience that is engaging and sparks interest for your target audience. Develop a clear strategy: Define your goals and the results you want to achieve. Establish a clear message and a clear call to action. Collaborating with influencers should be part of your overall marketing strategy and not just a single event. Choose different formats: Different formats such as videos, images or live streams can be used to convey the brand's message and reach your target audience. Analyze the results: Monitor the performance of the influencer campaign and measure how well it worked. Use analytics tools like Google Analytics or Social Media Analytics to track performance and optimize results. Overall, influencer marketing can be an effective way to promote the automotive industry. By following these steps, you can run a successful influencer campaign and reach your target audience effectively.

The pros and cons of influencer marketing

Influencer marketing is an important tool for promoting products or services and building trust among influencer followers. But as in every industry, there are certain dos and don'ts that should be taken into account. Here are some important points: Dos: Familiarize yourself with the legal framework: Many countries have legal requirements for influencer marketing. Find out what rules apply in your country so as not to risk legal consequences. Choose influencers that fit your product: Make sure that the influencers you work with target an audience that is relevant to your product or service. Create authentic content: Influencer marketing works best when the content is authentic. Give influencers enough freedom to add their own opinion and style to the content. Focus on long-term relationships: Long-term relationships with influencers can be beneficial for your business. They build trust among followers and can ensure repeat purchases. Measure success: Monitor the results of your influencer campaigns. Analyze what worked well and what didn't to optimize your future campaigns. Don'ts: Hide advertising: In many countries, the law requires advertising to be labeled as such. Don't hide advertising, label it clearly. Don't just focus on reach: High reach isn't everything. It is important that the influencer's target audience is relevant to your product. So pay attention not only to the number of followers, but also to their demographics and interests. Don't set false expectations: Make sure the products or services you promote deliver what they promise. Don't set false expectations to avoid negative reactions from followers. Don't go over budget: Influencer marketing can be expensive. Set a realistic budget and stick to it to avoid unnecessary spending. Ignore feedback: Listen to follower feedback. Take criticism seriously and respond to it. This shows that you care about what customers think and can help increase trust in your company.

The future of influencer marketing

Influencer marketing has become an important part of the marketing mix for many companies in recent years. However, there are some trends that suggest that influencer marketing will continue to evolve in the future: More regulation: Influencer marketing is a relatively new concept and there are still uncertainties surrounding the legal requirements. It is expected that regulation will increase in the future to encourage advertising disclosure and protect consumers. Focus on micro-influencers: While in the past the focus was often on large influencers with high follower numbers, in the future more companies will likely use micro-influencers who are active in a specific niche or topic and can therefore appeal to a narrower target group . Video content is becoming more important: Video content is already an important part of influencer marketing, but it will become even more important in the future. Platforms like TikTok and Instagram Reels have shown that short videos are becoming increasingly popular and that companies can use them to reach their audiences. Focus on authenticity: Consumers today are more demanding than ever and value authenticity. Influencers who have a real connection with their followers and are authentic will be more successful in the future. AI and data analytics: Artificial intelligence and data analysis will play a more important role in influencer marketing in the future. Companies can use AI to identify influencers who are a good fit for the brand and measure the success of campaigns. In summary, influencer marketing will continue to evolve in the future and companies that stay current and adapt will thrive.

Success stories in influencer marketing

There are many success stories in influencer marketing. Here are some examples: Daniel Wellington: Watch brand Daniel Wellington worked with influencers to promote their products. The collaboration was very successful and helped the brand build a large following in a short period of time. Glossier: Cosmetics brand Glossier used influencer marketing to promote their branding and products. The brand worked with many micro-influencers to reach its target audience. As a result, she achieved enormous success and became one of the most successful cosmetic brands on Instagram. Gymshark: Fitness brand Gymshark worked with influencers to promote their products and reach their target audience. Working with fitness influencers has been very successful and helped the brand build a large following. MVMT: Watch brand MVMT used influencer marketing to improve their branding and promote their products. The brand worked with many influencers to reach its target audience. As a result, it achieved enormous success and became one of the most successful watch brands on Instagram. SugarBearHair: The brand SugarBearHair used influencer marketing to promote their product, hair growth vitamin and supplements. The brand worked with many influencers to reach its target audience. As a result, she achieved enormous success and became one of the most successful nutritional supplement brands on Instagram. These success stories show that influencer marketing can be an effective way to promote products and brands and reach a target audience.

The best products for influencers

In general, the product groups are constantly changing. However, there are products that are often promoted by influencers such as: Beauty and skin care products Fitness and health products Fashion and jewelry items Technology products such as cell phones, cameras, tablets, etc. Food and beverages Travel and vacation packages Household products and home furnishings However, it is Important to note that influencers should act ethically and not promote products that do not align with their beliefs or benefit their followers. Additionally, they should always disclose clearly and honestly if they are being paid to promote a product. As an author, I do not have direct access to current sales figures for influencer products. However, I can tell you that influencers often promote and recommend products in the areas of fashion, beauty, fitness, nutrition and travel. Some of the most commonly promoted and recommended products by influencers include: Fashion items such as clothing, shoes and accessories from well-known brands and designers. Beauty products such as makeup, skin care products and hair care products from different brands. Fitness products such as protein shakes, nutritional supplements and fitness clothing from well-known brands. Nutritional products such as vegan or gluten-free foods, superfoods and nutritional supplements from various brands. Travel accessories such as suitcases, backpacks, cameras and travel clothing from various brands. It is important to note that the selection of products promoted by influencers can vary depending on the influencer, their target audience and the platform on which they are active.

Tax law regarding influencers

Influencers who earn income from their activities generally pay tax on this income. It is irrelevant whether the income comes from collaborations with companies or from other sources. As a rule, working as an influencer is classified as a commercial business for tax purposes. This means that the income must generally be reported on Appendix G of the income tax return. In addition, influencers can usually also claim advertising costs such as costs for the production of content or the purchase of equipment for tax purposes. If an influencer is resident in Germany, he or she is subject to German tax liability. Even if he is resident abroad but earns income in Germany, he may be subject to tax. There are also special tax regulations for influencers who promote company products or services. For example, advertising posts must be labeled as such to ensure transparency for viewers. In addition, influencers must ensure that no misleading advertising is used when promoting products. It is important that influencers take their tax obligations seriously and properly tax their income. If in doubt, you should contact a tax advisor to clarify your tax obligations as an influencer. Yes, there are special tax regulations for influencers who generate income from their activities. Influencers can work as self-employed entrepreneurs or as employees and must tax their income accordingly. The special tax regulations for influencers include: Business registration: Influencers who carry out their activities commercially must register a business and register with the tax office. VAT obligation: If the influencer's annual turnover is above a certain limit (22,000 euros in 2021), he or she is obliged to pay VAT and submit regular advance VAT returns. Deductibility of expenses: Influencers can deduct certain expenses such as equipment, office supplies, advertising or travel expenses from their taxes as business expenses. Tax recording of income: Influencers must declare their income from their activity in their tax return and tax it accordingly. Obligatory social insurance: Influencers who work as self-employed entrepreneurs usually have to take care of their own social insurance and pay contributions to health insurance, pension insurance and unemployment insurance. It is important that influencers find out about the tax regulations and obligations and comply with them carefully in order to avoid problems with the tax office. It is advisable to consult a tax advisor if you have any tax questions. Tax rates for influencers depend on various factors, including the country in which they are based, the nature of their activity and the level of their income. In most countries, influencers have to pay income taxes on their income. In the United States, the income tax rate for individuals up to a certain amount is 10%, 12%, 22%, 24%, 32%, 35% or 37%, depending on the amount of taxable income. Special tax rates apply to self-employed people in the USA, which can be higher than for employees. In Germany, the income tax rate for 2021 is 0% for single people with an income of up to 9,408 euros, 14% for incomes between 9,409 euros and 57,051 euros, 42% for incomes between 57,052 euros and 270,500 euros, and for incomes over 270,501 euros 45%. In other countries, tax rates may also be different. It is important that influencers research the tax regulations in their country and, if necessary, consult a tax advisor to ensure they are paying their taxes correctly.

Collaborate with other influencers

Collaborating with other influencers can be a very effective way to expand your audience and reach new audiences. Here are some tips that can help when collaborating with other influencers: Find suitable partners: Choose influencers who work in the same or a similar industry and appeal to a similar audience. Joint cooperation can be beneficial for both sides. Define the goal: Before you start collaborating, you should define the goal of the collaboration. For example, do you want to generate more reach or more engagement? Or do you want to promote a specific message or product? Clarify the details: Discuss all the details of the collaboration with your partner, such as the time frame, the type of cooperation and the distribution of tasks. Make sure both parties understand the expectations and requirements. Add value: Make sure the collaboration provides value to both influencers' viewers. For example, offers exclusive content or discounts to make collaboration more attractive. Be authentic: Authenticity is the key to success in the influencer industry. Collaborate with influencers who fit you and your audience and make sure the collaboration feels natural and authentic. Market the collaboration: Use social media and other channels to market the collaboration and make it visible to both influencers' audiences. If you keep these tips in mind, collaborating with other influencers can be a great way to expand your audience and increase your brand awareness.

Influencers and social projects

Influencers can play an important role in promoting social projects. Their reach and popularity allow them to draw attention to specific issues and encourage people to get involved in a good cause. Some influencers use their platform to directly raise funds for charities or to raise awareness for a specific cause. Other influencers work with nonprofit organizations to support and promote their projects. In some cases, influencers can also act as ambassadors for a specific cause or organization by publicly showing their support and encouraging people to get involved too. However, it is important to note that not all influencers who engage in social projects always have the best intentions. Some influencers may attempt to portray themselves as benefactors to increase their own popularity or to further their own agendas. It's important to assess an influencer's credibility and integrity before engaging with him or her. Overall, however, influencers can play a positive role in promoting social projects by using their reach to raise awareness and motivate people to support a good cause.

What basic knowledge is needed?

As an influencer, you need various techniques to establish a successful online presence and build a dedicated following. Here are some of the most important techniques: Social Media Knowledge: As an influencer, it is important to understand the different social media platforms and how to best use them. These include platforms such as Instagram, TikTok, YouTube, Twitter and Facebook. Content Creation: A successful influencer must be able to create high-quality and engaging content that appeals to their target audience. This can include photos, videos, blog posts, podcasts and more. Marketing Strategy: Influencers need to be able to market their content and reach their target audience. This includes techniques such as SEO, PPC, influencer marketing and other digital marketing methods. Creativity: Influencers must be able to be creative and come up with innovative ideas for their content and marketing strategies. Analytics Skills: To be successful, influencers must be able to measure and analyze the effectiveness of their content and marketing strategies to see what works and what doesn't. This includes knowledge of Google Analytics, social media analysis tools and other analysis methods. Communication: Influencers need to be able to communicate effectively with their audience and receive feedback to improve their content and marketing strategies. This includes skills such as social media management, community management and customer support. These techniques are just a few of the key skills a successful influencer needs to establish a strong online presence and build an engaged following.

What hardware is needed as an influencer

As an influencer, you usually need solid equipment to be able to produce high-quality content. However, the hardware required depends largely on the type of influencer marketing being done. For most influencers, a good camera and microphone are essential to producing high-quality photos, videos, and audio recordings. There are a variety of cameras and microphones in the market that can be selected according to your needs and budget. Some influencers also need a powerful computer to edit videos and photos, while others only need a smartphone to create and upload content. In addition to the camera and microphone, it may also be necessary to use various lighting equipment or background props to achieve the desired visual result. Another important factor is internet connection, as influencers typically spend a lot of time online and need to upload large files. A stable and fast internet connection is therefore essential. In summary, the hardware needed to be an influencer depends greatly on the type of influencer marketing being done, but a camera, microphone and a stable internet connection are usually essential.

Becoming an influencer as a child

Influencers are referred to as people who have a large number of followers on social media platforms such as Instagram, YouTube or TikTok and can be used by brands and companies for marketing purposes due to their reach and influence. There are some children who have become known as influencers due to their age and activity on social media platforms. However, it is important to note that children are typically unable to make decisions that can have long-term effects on their lives. This means they may not be able to fully understand the consequences and impact of their online activities. Additionally, the role of an influencer can be very demanding and requires a lot of work and commitment. Children may have to spend long hours creating content, building their reach and audience, and collaborating with brands and companies. It is important that parents and guardians take responsibility for preparing their children for online activities and supporting them in deciding whether they want to become influencers. It is also important to ensure that children are safe in their online activity and are not spreading inappropriate content or being presented in an inappropriate manner. Overall, it is possible for children to become influencers, but it is important that they have the support of their parents and guardians and that their safety and well-being always come first.

How much money can I earn

The amount of income an influencer can earn depends on many factors, such as: Number of followers: Typically, influencers with a larger number of followers make more money than those with a smaller number of followers. Niche: An influencer who is in a lucrative niche such as beauty, fashion, or fitness can typically earn more than someone who is in a less lucrative niche. Type of collaboration: The type of collaboration can also have a big impact on income. For example, influencers can earn money through paid posts, affiliate marketing, sponsorships, advertising deals or by creating their own products. Engagement rate: The engagement rate, i.e. the ratio of likes, comments and shares to the number of followers, is also an important factor. Influencers with a high engagement rate can make more money because they have an engaged and loyal fan base. According to a study by Influencer Marketing Hub, an influencer with fewer than 10,000 followers earns an average of $88 per post, while influencers with more than 1 million followers earn an average of $2,000 per post. However, influencers' income opportunities can vary greatly and depend on many factors. 38. Does the influencer only care about money It is not fair to say that all influencers only care about money, as each influencer has different motivations and goals. Some influencers enjoy building a community and interacting with other people, while others enjoy sharing their passions and interests with others. However, it is also true that many influencers want to live from their work and make money. This is particularly relevant if they make a living through social media platforms as it is a calling that requires a lot of work and effort. There are also some influencers who will do anything to make more money, including promoting products or services that they don't necessarily endorse. Ultimately, however, it is important to look at each influencer individually to understand what motivates and drives them.

Is influencer a profession

Yes, influencer can be considered a profession. An influencer is a person who has a large number of followers or subscribers on social media and has thereby established a significant online presence and reach. Influencers use their platform to promote products or services or to share their opinions and views. Influencers often make money through partnerships with brands, advertising, or by selling their own products or services. Working as an influencer often requires high activity on various social media channels, creating content, interacting with the community and maintaining relationships with brands and companies. However, it is important to note that being an influencer can also come with disadvantages, such as the pressure to always be present, the need to constantly be creative, and managing public feedback and criticism. 40. Final Thoughts and Summary Influencer marketing has gained significant traction in recent years and has a significant impact on consumers' purchasing decisions. The role of influencers is to promote products or services and motivate their followers to buy them. Influencers can be active on various social media platforms including Instagram, YouTube, TikTok and others. The choice of platform depends on the target group and the goals of the brand or company. Influencers need to build a loyal and engaged following by regularly creating high-quality, relevant content. This requires a lot of work, commitment and time. However, it is important that the collaboration between influencer and brand or company is transparent and authentic. Consumers value honesty and authenticity and are less inclined to buy products from influencers who only promote for commercial reasons. Overall, influencer marketing has its pros and cons, but when done carefully, it can be an effective marketing strategy for gaining consumer trust and loyalty.

Imprint / Copyright 2023

Luna Ludwig
Am Anger 3
06869 Coswig

Germany
Luna-Publishing.de